RADIANT RAINBOWS

First Edition
27 26 25 24 23   5 4 3 2 1

Published by
Gibbs Smith
P.O. Box 667
Layton, Utah 84041

1.800.835.4993 orders
www.gibbs-smith.com

Designers: Virginia Snow and Jessica Swift
Art director: Ryan Thomann
Editor: Kenzie Quist
Production editor: Sue Collier
Production manager: Felix Gregorio

Printed and bound in China by RR Donnelley Asia Printing Solutions

Gibbs Smith books are printed on either recycled, 100% post-consumer
waste, FSC-certified papers or on paper produced from sustainable PEFC-
certified forest/controlled wood source. Learn more at www.pefc.org.

Library of Congress Control Number: 2022941921

ISBN: 978-1-4236-6363-8

RADIANT RAINBOWS

MESSAGES OF HOPE, HEALING, AND COMFORT

Jessica Swift

Gibbs Smith

Life isn't easy.

We all encounter pain. Some people experience more pain and hardship; others experience less. Some people face the worst things you could imagine, while others' painful experiences are less dramatic. But none of us is immune to the reality that pain is part of life, and life is hard for everyone in one way or another.

On August 14, 2018, my husband Ryan died.

It was three days before my thirty-eighth birthday. Our first child was a month shy of three, and I was pregnant with our second child. Ryan was forty. A talented and compassionate doctor. A dad and a husband. A son and a brother. A skier and a woodworker. And he was deep in an addiction that didn't come to light until it was too late.

His death was unexpected and tragic. In that instant, I faced a completely unfamiliar and unimaginable future. I faced the unthinkable grief of losing a spouse. My world turned upside down in a second, and it was one of the worst things I could've imagined—heart-wrenching, traumatic, terrifying, sad, lonely, confusing, rage-inducing, and tear-soaked.

And yet. And yet!
I am okay. I am okay!
I am a tiger. I am resilient.

My grief was so all-encompassing in the immediate aftermath that I couldn't have contained it in my body even if I'd tried. The pain quickly started to teach me important lessons in my healing process. It was wild and uncontrollable. It was bigger than anything I'd ever felt before. And it showed me that if I just allowed it to flow through me—even though it hurt like hell—I would find myself on the other side of a wave, and then I would feel better. I just kept allowing the waves to flow and flow and flow. . . .

In the early days after Ryan's death, I created forty small rainbow paintings that I gave to family and close friends. I don't know why I felt called to paint rainbows, but it felt comforting and intuitively "right." Ryan's mom, my mother-in-law, also naturally resonated with rainbows during this time, and the serendipities between us were surprising, magical, and meaningful. Rainbows were a way to remember Ryan and to connect us all during this tremendously painful time. Painting them was soothing, and it was something that my mind and my hands could focus on. As I painted, the rainbows morphed for me and started to symbolize the profound gratitude I felt for the outpouring of love and support I was receiving. I learned that gratitude and grieving could exist within me simultaneously. Rainbows are now a significant and recurring symbol in my work.

Rainbows remind me that inside the mess, there's a lot of beauty. They remind me that beauty can't exist without messiness. They're not different things; they're cosmically intertwined. Light and dark. Pain and joy. Fear and courage. Same same same.

Pain holds gifts.
Pain contains lessons.
Pain will break you into pieces, and then put you back together better and wiser than before, if you let it.
Pain grows you.
Shapes you.
Transforms you.

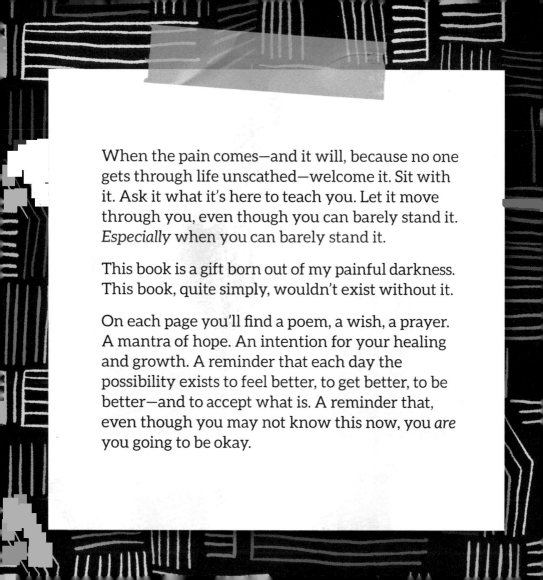

When the pain comes—and it will, because no one gets through life unscathed—welcome it. Sit with it. Ask it what it's here to teach you. Let it move through you, even though you can barely stand it. *Especially* when you can barely stand it.

This book is a gift born out of my painful darkness. This book, quite simply, wouldn't exist without it.

On each page you'll find a poem, a wish, a prayer. A mantra of hope. An intention for your healing and growth. A reminder that each day the possibility exists to feel better, to get better, to be better—and to accept what is. A reminder that, even though you may not know this now, you *are* you going to be okay.

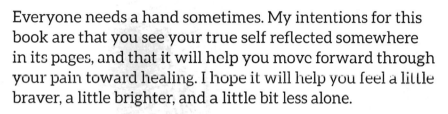

Everyone needs a hand sometimes. My intentions for this book are that you see your true self reflected somewhere in its pages, and that it will help you move forward through your pain toward healing. I hope it will help you feel a little braver, a little brighter, and a little bit less alone.

There is no cure for being human, and sometimes that's a difficult pill to swallow. These are my wishes for you as you navigate the precarious terrain of life as a fragile, strong, imperfectly perfect human.

Love,

LOVE

WORTHINESS

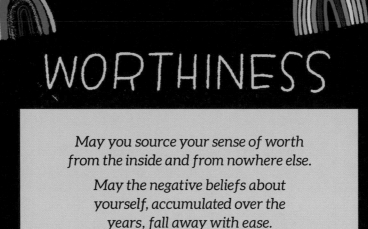

May you source your sense of worth
from the inside and from nowhere else.

May the negative beliefs about
yourself, accumulated over the
years, fall away with ease.

And may only the truest truths
be left—you were born worthy.
And you are worthy still.

No proof or measuring up
of any kind required.

BELONGING

*May you make a beautiful
home within yourself.*

May you always stay by your own side.

*May you abandon yourself
for nothing and no one.*

*May you see that the universe would
not be the same without you.*

*May you look within and see
the miracle that you are.*

COMPASSION

May you go easy on yourself.

*May you see yourself with gentle
eyes and a forgiving heart.*

*May you see that others are also traveling a hard
road and meet them with acceptance and care.
May you offer love when it feels the most difficult.*

May you radiate kindness.

PERMISSION

May you allow yourself to show up exactly as you are.

May you do things your own way, even if they are different.

May you give yourself space to change your mind.

May you let yourself live in the in-between,
where it's okay not to know all the answers.

May you welcome happiness inside your being.

KINDNESS

May you think kind thoughts.
May you use kind words.
May you do kind deeds.
May your heart be kind.
May your kindness radiate and ripple, inward and outward.
Inward and outward, inward and outward. . . .

EMPATHY

*May you meet others' heaviness
with reverence and kindness.*

*May you bravely sit in the dark with someone
who is in need of a loving hand to hold.*

*May your capacity for care help
to lighten someone's load.*

May you listen without judgment.

May your presence be of supreme comfort.

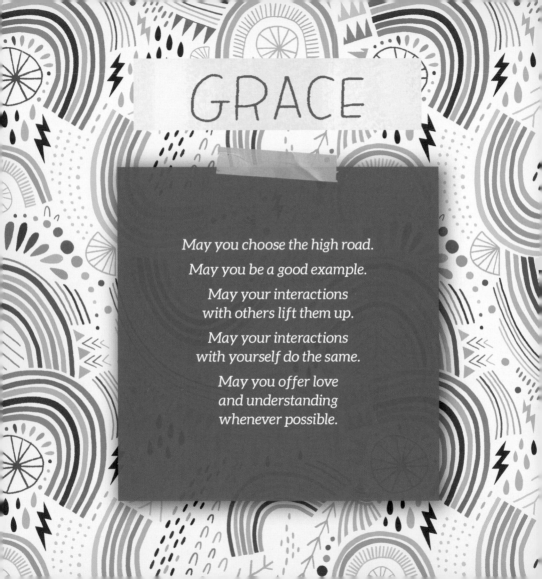

GRACE

May you choose the high road.

May you be a good example.

May your interactions with others lift them up.

May your interactions with yourself do the same.

May you offer love and understanding whenever possible.

FORGIVENESS

May you accept what was and allow what is.

May you gaze gently upon yourself and others with kind eyes and a forgiving heart.

May you forgive because you deserve peace inside your heart.

INTUITION

FEELING

May you cultivate the ability to watch your feelings move through you like a wave.

May you courageously sit through the hard waves.

May you enjoy the fleeting, beautiful ones.

May you know that conflicting emotions can coexist.

Gratitude and grieving. Relief and rage. Hope and misery.

May you allow it all, without fear or judgment.

LISTENING

May your heart be your guide.

*May your loving inner voice speak
louder and more persuasively
than the voice of fear.*

*May you hear the words
within that lift you up and
dismiss the ones that don't.*

*May the beautiful truth of
who you really are resonate
and hum deep within you.*

QUIET

May you find rest.

May you find ease.

May you find the space you crave and the silence you require to hear the deepest whisperings of your soul.

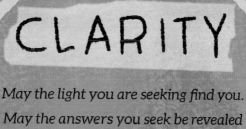

CLARITY

May the light you are seeking find you.

May the answers you seek be revealed to you in their own perfect right time.

May your wise inner voice guide you toward vast inner riches.

May confusion give way to sureness.

May your vision be clear and unshakable.

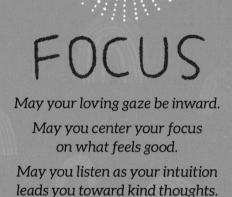

FOCUS

May your loving gaze be inward.

*May you center your focus
on what feels good.*

*May you listen as your intuition
leads you toward kind thoughts.*

Away from negativity, bit by bit.

*May gratitude fill your mind
and your heart with ease.*

PEACE

May you breathe in peace and breathe out fear.

May you experience calm in the midst of chaos.

*May you create an inner sanctuary
where you are always safe and loved.*

May your soul be light and free.

TRUST

May your inner eye be your most
potent and powerful tool for navigating your life.
May you know that the truest you, the wise one that lives deep
within, only speaks to you kindly and wants nothing but the best for you.
May you trust that listening to your intuition and following its
guidance will always lead you in the direction you're meant to go.

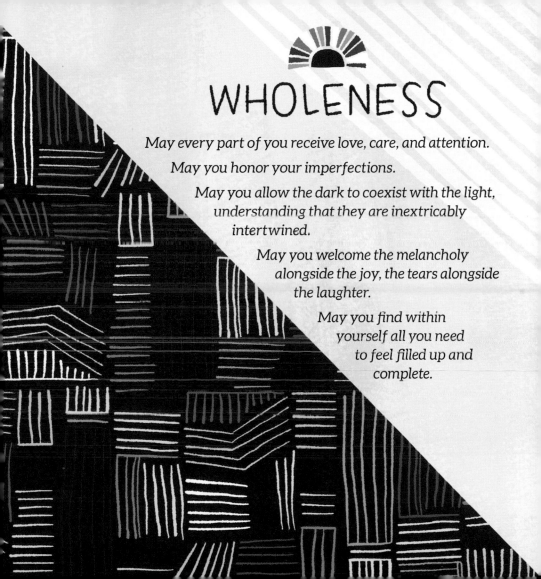

WHOLENESS

May every part of you receive love, care, and attention.

May you honor your imperfections.

May you allow the dark to coexist with the light, understanding that they are inextricably intertwined.

May you welcome the melancholy alongside the joy, the tears alongside the laughter.

May you find within yourself all you need to feel filled up and complete.

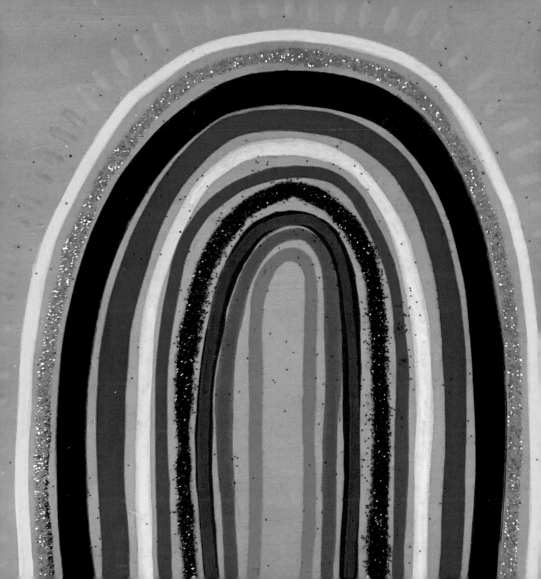

COURAGE

VULNERABILITY

May your heart stay open.

May you face the hardest things with courage and tears and allow them to expand your capacity for love and understanding.

May you free your body of bottled-up feelings.

May you share the story of you— raw, real, honest, and true.

AUDACITY

*May you dare to follow your heart and
your own inner voice at all costs.*

*May you willingly take bold risks and chances in
service of creating your best and most beautiful life.*

*May you see fear and pain and courageously
move forward in spite of it all.*

*May you follow your values and not be
swayed by pressure from others.*

*May you see good where others see darkness.
May you be light when others are heavy.
May you create love where there is none.*

ADVENTURE

May you be curious.

*May the truth that everything is working out
in your favor guide you forward.*

*May you see the value in every experience you encounter.
Even the painful ones. Especially the painful ones.*

*May you greet each day with curious enthusiasm
for all that could be and all that already is.*

*May you say yes to the calling of
your heart. Yes yes YES.*

BRAVERY

*May you choose from love
and not from fear.*

*May you find the courage
within to stay when
you need to stay.*

*Go when you
need to go.*

*Say what you
need to say.*

*Be who you
are at all costs.*

*May you
stand up for
what is good
and right
and true.*

*May you
make yourself
proud.*

STRENGTH

May you unearth the strength to keep going
in the face of all that feels unbearable.

May you know the peace that comes with not
knowing what comes next but of also knowing that
you were made for this and that you will be okay.

May you believe that you have
what it takes to keep going.

You will be okay.
You will be okay.
You will be okay.

BOUNDARIES

May your priority be your own inner peace.

May self-love and self-respect be your north star.

*May you know what you will tolerate,
and also what you won't.*

You get to choose how others treat you.

You get to choose how you treat yourself.

*May you see that your life is for
you, and not for anyone else.*

May you choose well.

OPENNESS

May you refuse to become jaded.

May your loving heart shine
in spite of all it's endured.

May you believe that love
always wins over darkness.

May your heart's limitless capacity for
love keep you wide open and steady.

TENACITY

*May your pursuit of lightness and healing
powerfully guide your way forward.*

May you persist, and persist, and persist.

May your struggles propel you forward.

*May you continue to rise in the face of all
that has threatened to bring you down.*

*May you prove to yourself that
you have what it takes.*

You were made for this.

WILLINGNESS

May you show up.

May you keep showing up.

*May you gracefully take what life hands
you and find a way to handle it all.*

*May you allow life to change you
and transform you profoundly.*

May you let go and move forward with ease.

EXPANSION

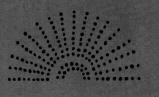

AWAKENING

May you wake up.

*May your perspective shift
and your perception alter.*

*May you allow the stories and beliefs
that keep you small to disintegrate.*

*May a wider, clearer view and
a deeper, truer you rise through
the fading mist of the illusion.*

TRANSFORMATION

*May you look back at past versions of yourself
and feel proud of how far you've come.*

*May you celebrate all your previous selves,
and also the current version of you.*

*May you welcome the next chapter
with curiosity and optimism.*

You get endless new beginnings.

*May each one bring you closer to
your most authentic you.*

GROWTH

May you feel that your heart is an ocean—limitless, wild, and free in its capacity to love and to feel and to grow.

May your heart expand with each joy and with each painful moment that you experience.

May you always look for and find the silver linings and the lessons.

May you believe that everything is working out in your favor, and for that reason every experience holds value and opportunities to grow and change and heal.

May you stay curious. May you stay open.

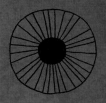

CREATIVITY

*May you let go of black and white and
live inside the messy grey.*

May your imagination lead you to surprising solutions.

*May your originality lead you in the
direction of your deepest desires.*

May you shine.

May you shine.

May you shine.

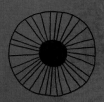

POSSIBILITY

May your imagination be powerfully alive.

May the beliefs that hold you back fade into the background and disappear completely.

You are the chooser. The decider.

May you believe the best. Choose the best.

May "I can do this" be your most potent prayer.

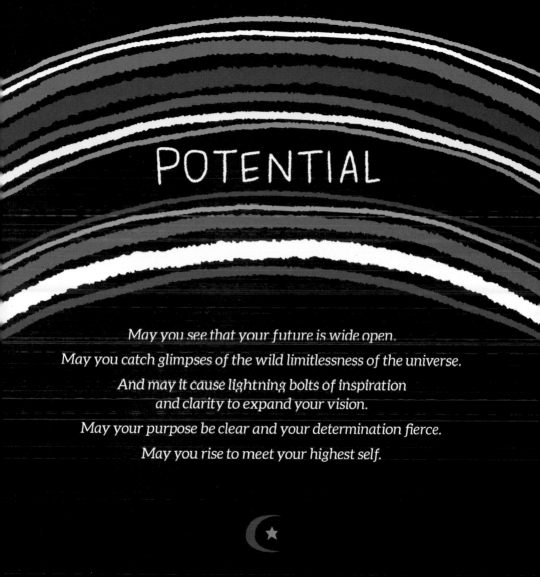

POTENTIAL

May you see that your future is wide open.

May you catch glimpses of the wild limitlessness of the universe.

And may it cause lightning bolts of inspiration
and clarity to expand your vision.

May your purpose be clear and your determination fierce.

May you rise to meet your highest self.

SHEDDING LAYERS

*May you let go of the outdated beliefs
that are no longer true or needed.*

*May your outgrown skin fall away with
ease to reveal the newest version of yourself.*

*May you let go and let go and let go
until all that is left is the bright shining
diamond deep in your core: YOU.*

Beautiful and whole in the center of it all.

FREEDOM

May you be free to change your mind.

Change your course.

Change your life.
May your mind not hold you hostage.

May you have the privilege of
making your own choices.

May you have everything
you need—and more.

RESILIENCE

WALKING THROUGH IT

*May you hold onto the belief that one
day you will be on the other side.*

May you do the next right thing. And then the one after that.

*May you look across the ravine between where you are
and where you wish you were in your healing and trust
that even though you cannot see a bridge, there is a bridge.*

May you believe that you will be held in your crossing.

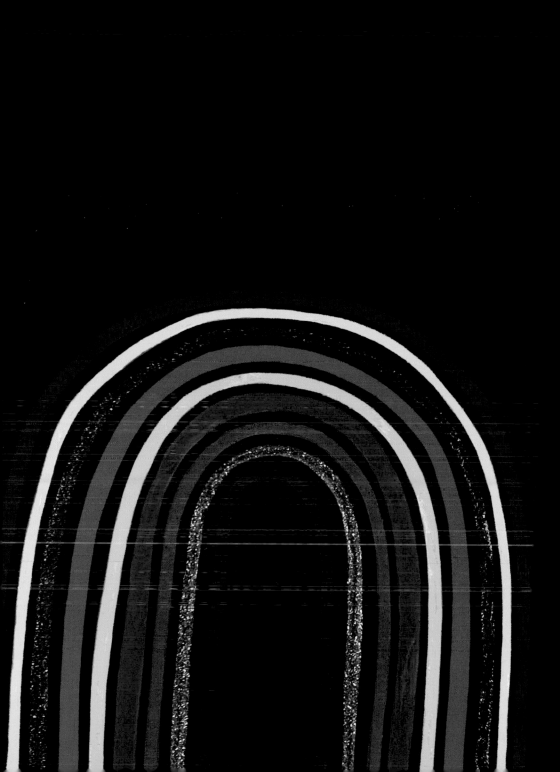

HOPE

May you, even in your darkest hour, believe that it's possible for things to get better.

May you persist when you feel defeated.

May you carry on when you want to give up.

May the fire within you always stay lit.

And may love
always,
always
win.

PRESENCE

*May a peaceful acceptance of
yourself and your life fill your being.*

*May you trust that, right now, you are
exactly where you are meant to be.*

*May you appreciate all that you
have and all that you are.*

*May you find safety and comfort
in the okay-ness of this moment.*

ADAPTABILITY

May you welcome change, not fear it.

May you continue to rise up each time you fall.

*May you reinvent yourself as
many times as you need to.*

*May you pivot with grace, face what
comes, and know that you have what it
takes to make your way through it all.*

You were made for this.

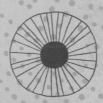

RELIEF

May anxiety leave your body.

May you feel freedom from distress.

May you find reassurance and comfort.

May the burden of heaviness lighten.

May peace flood in and fear evaporate.

AUTHENTICITY

May your true essence shine through
you and add light to the world.

May your soul's calling speak to you
freely, loudly, and persuasively.

May you do things your own way
and enjoy your own company.

May honoring your true self
be a sacred commitment.

May you feel free to be exactly who you are.

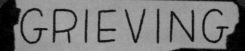

GRIEVING

*May you allow the heaviness to
exist without trying to push it away.*

*May you sit courageously in the
uncomfortable pain of it all.*

*May you allow the pain to change you.
When you do, you will not be the same.*

*You will be better for it, though
that's difficult to imagine right now.*

May your heart grow deeper and wider.

May you be tender with your wounded spirit.

WISDOM

May you glean the lessons and
the gifts from your pain.

(They are there.)

May you allow your pain to crack you wide open,
and may you use it to put yourself back together.
The same you, but also not the same you at all.

May you use the gifts from your hard-earned
lessons to light the way forward for others.

May you see that everyone is a
teacher, everyone is a guide.

INTEGRATION

May every past version of yourself live sweetly in your heart.

*May you see that you would not be who you
are now without who you were then.*

*May your dreams and your regrets
coexist peacefully within you.*

*May you welcome the shadows and the
sunshine in order to create wholeness.*

May you send love to every single part of yourself.

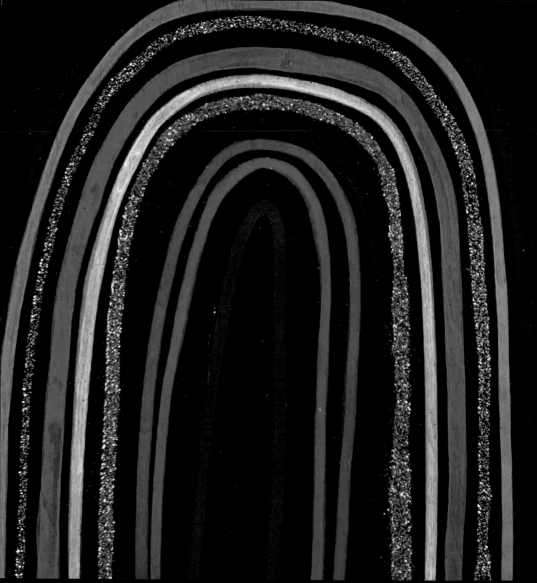

RADICAL ACCEPTANCE

SURRENDER

*May you choose in this moment
to melt into something higher.*

Something sacred.

Something unknowable, deep, vast, and wide.

*May you know that surrender is
not giving up or giving in.*

*Surrender is flowing downstream.
It is trust in place of resistance.*

*It is an allowing of what is, which will lead
you to exactly where you are meant to be.*

ALLOWING

May you accept that even though this moment may not be what you want, it is what you have.

May you allow things to simply be as they are—without any story, without resistance, without judgment.

May you simply observe the truth of what is and appreciate the sacred, quiet, beautiful mess of this precious moment that never will exist again.

LETTING GO

May you let go of expectations of how things should be in order to see clearly and embrace things as they are.

May you forgive.

May you carry on without the weight of all that is holding you down.

May you let go to lift up.

Let go to lift up.

Let go to lift up.

NEW BEGINNINGS

May every ending also be an invitation.

A fresh start. A new perspective.

May you embrace the next chapter, even while grieving the last.

May you allow yourself the space to begin . . .

Again and again and again, as many times as you need.

FAITH

*May you trust the
timing of your life.*

*May you believe that everything
is working out in your favor
(even though it might not
always feel that way).*

*May your belief in yourself be
stronger than your doubt and
your confidence unwavering.*

DESERVINGNESS

May you know that your worth is inherent.

May you feel equal, important, and valuable.

May you zoom out into space, looking down
at the earth, to see that you belong here.

Just as much as everyone else.

May you know that your feelings matter.

Your happiness matters.

YOU matter.

GRATITUDE

· ·

*May you stand at the still point between where you were
then and where you will end up and say thank you.*

May the sacredness of all things flow through you like gold.

May you remember the truth of your fragile existence.

May you greet the day with wonder and reverence.

*May you find the holy value in it all—the pain,
the joy, and all the messy in-between.*

· ·

TELLING THE TRUTH

May you speak what's true and find freedom.

May your desire for freedom and
inner peace outweigh your fear.

May your fear guide you to shame-
filled, ugly dark shadowy corners.

And may you courageously shine light of truth there.

And everywhere.

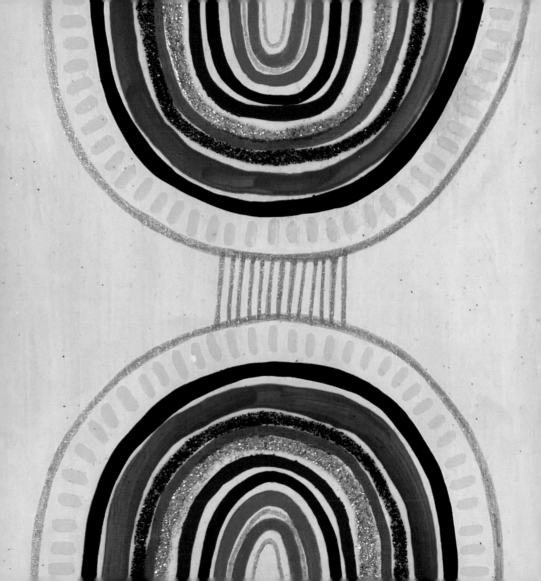

ALCHEMY

May you turn your pain into gold.

*May you be forged in the fire and
come out stronger and shining
more brightly than before.*

*May you transform your heaviness into
a gift for yourself and for the world.*

May your teardrops lead to rainbows.

May magic find you each step of the way.

JOY

May you stand in awe of the miracle
of your life in this moment.

May you pursue your own pleasure without guilt.

May you seek and find the rainbows
in the middle of all the mess.

May the universe hold you, and may you
marvel at its wild, complex beauty.

REVERENCE

*May you witness the sacred beauty of your
life in this wild and precious moment.*

*May you feel the vibrations all around
you and drink in the wild beauty of it all.*

*May the mundane moments be
infused with love and magic.*

May your life be a prayer, a poem, a gift.

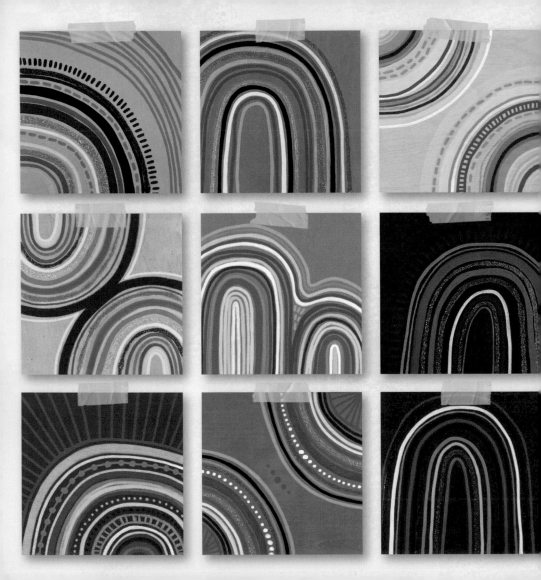

MIRACLES

*May the universe hold
you, and may you feel it.*

*May everything fall into
place in exactly the right way
at exactly the right time.*

May you let go and trust.

Let go and trust.

May your life contain magic.

FIERCENESS

May you be forged in the fire.

*May you mean what you say,
and say what you mean.*

*May you believe in goodness,
even when life has broken you.*

*And refuse to give up when
life knocks you down.*

*May you, through your hardship,
discover a stronger and more
resilient version of yourself.*

Fire cannot burn this.

MANIFESTATION

May you let go of anything that stands
in the way of creating your best life.

May you dream the best for yourself.

May your imagination guide
you toward contentment.

May you align yourself with true deservingness.

May you feel worthy of all you desire.

POWER

May you claim space.

May you respect others and also yourself.

May you know that true power comes from within; it's not about gaining power over others.

May you have compassion and be a vessel through which the universe can work and flow.

May you remember that we are all one and act accordingly.

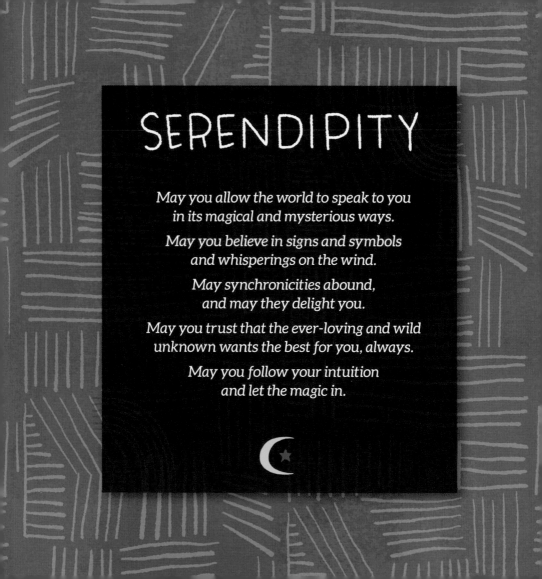

SERENDIPITY

*May you allow the world to speak to you
in its magical and mysterious ways.*

*May you believe in signs and symbols
and whisperings on the wind.*

*May synchronicities abound,
and may they delight you.*

*May you trust that the ever-loving and wild
unknown wants the best for you, always.*

*May you follow your intuition
and let the magic in.*

SELF-LOVE

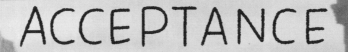

ACCEPTANCE

May you see that you are always doing the best you can.

May you allow that to be enough.

May you honor your imperfect perfection. Everyone is this way.

May you believe in your bones that you are enough.

You are enough.
You are enough.
You are enough.

APPRECIATION

May you hold yourself in the highest regard.

May you marvel at the wonder of your unique being. There is no one else like you.

May you offer love to yourself how you would offer it to someone you hold dear.

May you feel connected to yourself.

May your inner world be a peaceful and loving home.

CONFIDENCE

May you value yourself as much as you value others.

May you be bold and courageous in speaking what's true, regardless of others' views.

May your opinion of yourself matter to you the most.

May your trust in yourself be firm and certain.

SELF-RELIANCE

*May you lovingly excavate all your inner
corners until you are unshakable to your core.*

*May you know without any doubt that,
no matter what, you will always be okay.*

May you abandon all self-doubt.

*May you trust that the answers you
seek exist within yourself already.*

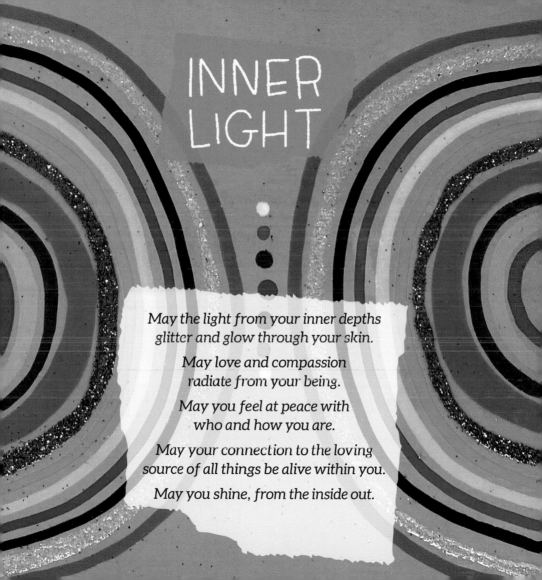

INNER LIGHT

*May the light from your inner depths
glitter and glow through your skin.*

*May love and compassion
radiate from your being.*

*May you feel at peace with
who and how you are.*

*May your connection to the loving
source of all things be alive within you.*

May you shine, from the inside out.

INNER BEAUTY

May you feel at home in the wilds of the mysterious unknown.
May you meet yourself with loving care and deep care.
May you witness your inner glow when looking in the mirror.
May you delight in the miracle that you are alive.

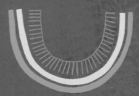

SOVEREIGNTY

*May your actions align with the
wishes of your highest soul self.*

*May you take full responsibility for how
you show up in life. And may it set you free.*

*May your ability to depend on
yourself be of powerful comfort.*

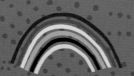

As a child, **Jessica Swift** sported a nearly permanent Crayola marker stain on her left arm, from pinky to elbow. She grew up and, naturally, became an artist. Jessica creates colorful, uplifting artwork and manufactures her own products in her studio in Portland, Oregon.

She also collaborates with inspiring companies and publishers to create branded products such as fabrics, stationery, puzzles, books, and more. Two rambunctious, creative young children call her mama.

You can find Jessica on her website at www.jessicaswift.com and follow her on Instagram @jessicaswift.